CROFTS AND CROFTING

CROFTS
AND
CROFTING

KATHARINE STEWART

1804

William Blackwood
Edinburgh

William Blackwood
32 Thistle Street
Edinburgh EH2 1HA

First published 1980
© Katharine Stewart 1980

ISBN 0 85158 137 4

Printed by William Blackwood & Sons Ltd

Contents

Bibliography

Carmina Gadelica, Alexander Carmichael.

The Future of the Highlands, Ed. Derick C. Thomson and Ian Grimble (Routledge & Kegan Paul 1968).

Hebridean Islands—Colonsay, Gigha, Jura, John Mercer (Blackie, 1974).

Highland Folk Ways, I. F. Grant (Routledge & Kegan Paul, 1961).

The Making of the Crofting Community, James Hunter (John Donald, 1976).

Reminiscences of an Orkney Parish, John Firth (Stromness, 1974).

Scottish Country Life, Alexander Fenton (John Donald, 1976).

To the people of the crofts,
whose friendship I prize–
agus mo bheannachdan
agus mo mhile taing
dhaibh uile.

Crofting lands

PREDOMINANT

MIXED WITH FARMING

SOURCE:
H A Moisley —
trans. Inst. Br. Geogr.
© HIDB 1976

Reproduced with the kind permission of the Highlands and Islands Development Board.

What is a Croft?

A crofter's son once defined a croft as a small area of land entirely surrounded by regulations. A brief look at the history of the crofting system will make clear the need and the reason for the regulations. The word 'croft', comes from the Gaelic *coirtean*, meaning a small, enclosed field. The significance of this derivation will become evident when considering how ways of holding land evolved in what came to be known as 'the crofting counties', the former counties of Shetland, Orkney, Caithness, Sutherland, Ross and Cromarty, Inverness and Argyll.

In very early times, before the emergence of the clans, there was a belief that lengthy occupation gave right to a 'kindness', or permanency of settlement, though not actual ownership, of land. This belief persisted into the modern age; the commission appointed in 1884 to inquire into the grievances of the crofters said: 'This opinion was often expressed before us—that the small tenantry of the Highlands have an inherited, inalienable title to security of tenure in their possessions while rent and service are duly rendered is an impression indigenous to the country, though it has never been sanctioned by legal recognition and has long been repudiated by the action of the proprietors.' Also from those early days dates the belief that the Highlander has the right to take a stag from the hill, a salmon from the pool and a tree from the wood—an idea which dies hard!

There is no doubt that this feeling of close affinity with the natural world is a mark of the Celt. It finds expression in the marvellous fertility of the Gaelic language which has, for example, over a dozen different words for an area of high ground, according to whether: the ground rises sharply and is very high (*bean*); is rounded (*meall* or *ord*); is less high and pointed (*ard*) or ridged (*druim*); is a small hillock (*cnoc*); is a slope (*leitir*); is rocky and steep (*aoineadh*) or rocky and flat (*carn*). Then there are others—*tor, tom, creag, dun, brae.* This feeling of affinity is also apparent in the largely urbanised world of today; so many exiles travel half round the globe to see the hills and lochs so graphically named—'the cold, wet hill' or 'the loch of the white eagle'—by their forebears.

The Celts known as Scots came from Ireland during the fifth century and settled in what became Argyllshire, forming a colony which they called Dalriada. There were already Britons in the Clyde valley, while to the north and east the Picts were in control and threatened many times to overrun the small kingdom of the Scots. However, in the year 864 the King of the Scots, Kenneth Macalpine, succeeded to the throne of the Picts, and Gaelic culture then came to dominate the whole kingdom of Alba, as Scotland was then called. Land was held in common and was considered to belong to the tribe.

Meanwhile, the Norsemen were conquering and settling in large areas of the Western Isles and the mainland, as the many place names of Norse origin testify. They were not culturally as advanced as the Gaels and did not succeed in obliterating Celtic civilisation.

The Gaelic kingdom survived, but under the rule of Malcolm Canmore and his successors (1057-1289) southern influences became important and the social structure of Scotland was drastically changed as the feudal system of landholding was introduced. Large grants of land were made to incomers from the south, many of them of Norman blood. A new concept of the legal rights to land developed. It was no longer in the possession of the tribe. The king was considered its owner with power to grant lots by charter to certain of his subjects in return for specific dues, including military service. A 'barony', for instance, was the amount of land expected to provide the service of an armed and mounted man.

After the wars of independence which Scotland waged against England between 1296 and 1314 much land held by the pro-English was made forfeit and reallocated to Scottish patriots. This was an important factor in the growth of clan society. The word clan is the Gaelic *clann,* meaning children. Land allocated to a king's favourite passed to his children and his children's children. It was essentially an aristocratic society, and each member of the clan claimed kinship with the chief. As time went on, inter-clan warfare developed and it was in the interest of the chief to have a numerous following. The clan was extended to include all those who acknowledged the authority of a chief and accepted his protection. It is said that a Fraser of Lovat offered the bribe of a boll of meal to any of his tenants who would take his name. Those who accepted were known as 'boll o' meal' Frasers.

The chief saw to the welfare of the members of the clan, administered justice and provided for the dependants of those who had given good service. The clansmen were 'tenants at will' and could be moved about, but it was understood that they would always be provided with land. By the seventeenth century a chief with a well-established territory often gave a permanent lease of land to a son or other close relative. These tenants were known as 'tacksmen' and were responsible for the military organisation of the clan. They sublet most of their land, many of them living comfortably off their tenants. These tenants worked the land in groups, as joint cultivators, in a system known as 'run-rig'. The arable was apportioned in strips, which were balloted for each year, so that everyone had a share in the good land and in the poorer. There were also people known as 'cottars' who paid no rent and had no land allotted to them, but who helped in the work of cultivation in return for subsistence.

The tenants themselves earned little more than bare subsistence. Their houses were poor and comfortless, often built of turf, though sometimes of stone, with thatched roofs. The peat fire was laid on the floor in the middle of the main room and was never extinguished, the smoke issuing from a small hole in the roof. Hens roosted on the rafters and, in winter, the cattle were housed at one end of the building. These cattle were the mainstay of the economy. Oats and bere, a kind of barley, were used for human consumption. A good milk cow was, obviously, a most precious possession as a provider of milk, butter and cheese. Only a few sheep were kept, to provide wool for clothing, an occasional dish of stew and sometimes milk. Goats often ran with the sheep.

Despite the hardships of a life spent trying to coax a harsh land to yield the milk and honey which they craved, the people felt secure in their kinship with one another and with their chief. Often a chief's son would be fostered in a clansman's family. All were assured of a rough and ready justice meted out by the head of the clan in any dispute. They had confidence in their skills as herdsmen and cultivators. The women had acquired the arts of spinning and dyeing wool and had a knowledge of herbal cures and specifics. The poems and songs which have come down to us from these earlier times tell of people sensitive to their world in all its aspects, living a close-knit communal life and passionately attached to their glens and hills.

In the course of the eighteenth century, after the union with England and when communications were developing, the Highland chiefs began to absent themselves more frequently from their lands. A new world of opportunity and ease was opening up to them. As roads were improved and bridges built, regular contact could be maintained with all parts of the country and goods and ideas exchanged. The Highland area was no longer a fastness. However, social life in the south demanded money which the chiefs, as clan patriarchs, found difficulty in raising. They were obliged to begin thinking of ways to make their lands commercially profitable.

The Jacobite rebellions ended in the defeat of the Highlanders at Culloden in 1746. Then followed the destruction of the clan as a military organisation threatening the stability of the state, and the attempt to modernise the Highland economy. Modernisation meant supplying the

needs of the developing industries of England and Lowland Scotland. Black cattle formed the traditional export of the Highlands. Now it was discovered that two other valuable commodities could be produced—wool and kelp—so leading to the establishment of the small individual holdings which have become known as 'crofts'.

Kelp-making, that is the burning of seaweed to produce alginate used in the manufacture of glass and soap, needed a large labour force. People were therefore offered the inducement of a small portion of land for their individual use, and a share in a common grazing, to get them to work for a small wage at the kelping. Twenty tons of wrack were needed to produce one ton of ash. It was seasonal work, the weed being gathered at low tide in the summer and brought to the shore to be burnt in peat-fired kilns. Many of the workers suffered severely from physical exhaustion and from rheumatism owing to being continuously wet. The lairds found a very profitable trade during the Napoleonic wars but, when peace came, barilla was imported from Spain and the Highland trade in kelp collapsed.

The lairds had to look to other ways of making money from their estates. Large areas were now let to sheep-farmers who kept the southern mills supplied with wool. The coming of the big sheep—*na caoraich mora*—meant that, inevitably, many small tenants were displaced. Emigration had been discouraged by the passing of the Passenger Shipping Act of 1803, which made the business costly when men were needed for the Army and for work at the kelping. Now it was the only way—some voluntary, much of it forced. The evictions, many carried out with thoughtless cruelty, have become known as the Clearances. People whose ancestors had lived for centuries in sheltered glens were expected to adapt to life on a small plot of land on a rocky coast. This could be said to be an attempt to develop fishing, but it bore hard on those who had never before set eyes on the sea.

So it was that, with the development of the kelp and fishing industries and the leasing of the good hill land to sheep-farmers, the croft as we know it still today—that is, the small individual holding of enclosed land, with a share in a common grazing—came into being in the early nineteenth century. The acreage of the croft was deliberately kept low, so that the occupant would engage in other money-making work which would benefit his landlord, as the clan chief had now become, in the form of rent. (This is a situation which still exists, though the ancillary work which the crofter engages in today may not necessarily benefit his landlord.)

But as the kelp industry declined and fishing fluctuated, the crofter was left on his smallholding with no means of paying his rent. It is little wonder that, with no kind of security, his initiative and enterprise were stifled. If he made improvements to his land by enclosing, draining, or putting up additional buildings, his rent was increased. He did what he could to improve his lot by hiring out himself and members of his family as reapers on the big farms in the south. Inevitably, his own small farm suffered from neglect. The land was becoming congested as holdings, already small, were subdivided to accommodate a growing population (early marriages were encouraged by the system of individual holdings) and the fertility of the soil was decreasing. As one Skye crofter put it in his beautiful, precise English, 'The smallness of the crofts renders it imperative on us to till the whole of our ground from year to year, and by so doing the land is growing inferior and less productive.'

Then, in 1846, came the famine caused by the failure of the potato crop on which so many families had come to depend for sustenance. This did, at least, bring the plight of the crofting population to the notice of various authorities. A board was set up to try to relieve the wretchedness by providing food and work in the making of what came to be known as the 'destitution roads'. Some lairds also helped by distributing meal and other foodstuffs, but nothing was done to reach the root cause of the trouble: not enough land was made available to provide the people with even part of their living. So the only solution was, again, emigration. There is no doubt that, in this way, many of the most able and enterprising families were lost to the Highlands for good. But a fight was soon to be engaged in to improve the lot of those who did not go.

The Land Wars

The visitor to Skye today, enjoying the peace and beauty of the island, would find it hard to visualise the scenes of violence which happened there in the early 1880s. Events of the same sort were occurring in other crofting areas, but those in Skye were particularly distressing.

During the 1870s there had been a rise in beef prices which had led to a certain amount of stability in crofting economy. The setting up of sporting establishments—shooting and fishing lodges—was providing some employment for men as stalkers and gillies and for women as domestic servants. Many sons and daughters still preferred to go south for the harvesting, though much of this was now done by Irish workers. The herring fishing also absorbed a good deal of seasonal labour. As a money economy became established, less time was spent on working the crofts and the land became less and less fertile. The crofter felt more intensely than ever the insecurity of his tenure and was even more reluctant to make improvements to his holding.

In 1873 John Murdoch of Inverness had founded a newspaper—the *Highlander*—in an attempt to make the crofters' grievances known. He addressed meetings, collected funds and persuaded, with difficulty, some of those hard-done-by to protest. Gladstone's Irish Land Act of 1881 had given security of tenure and judicially determined rents to small farmers in Ireland. Encouraged by articulate sympathisers in the Lowlands and by the utterances of the radical Press, the people of the Scottish Highlands began to stir.

B

At Martinmas 1881 the tenants of Braes in Skye marched in Portree to declare their refusal to pay their rents until the grazing on Ben Lee, which had been given over to the landlord's sheep, and on which their livelihood depended, was restored to them. The following April the sheriff officer went to serve eviction orders on a dozen tenants. He was accosted by a crowd of a hundred and fifty and the summonses were burned. Five crofters were arrested. The situation was so alarming that Sheriff Ivory of Inverness-shire asked for assistance from the Glasgow constabulary in restoring order. Before dawn on 19 April, a bitterly cold, wet day, fifty policemen, with Sheriff Ivory in the rear, set off from Portree to march to Braes. Taken by surprise, the people were thrown into confusion, but some managed to rally on the hillside, whence they rushed at the police, stoning them in desperation. Several arrests were made. This encounter became known as the Battle of the Braes. Many journalists were present and the accounts they submitted to their papers gave wide publicity to the crofters' cause. The arrested men were treated sympathetically by the authorities in Inverness, were given small fines and came home as heroes. Sheriff Ivory was refused military help, for which he hoped, but the police force was strengthened by fifty constables.

In the following October a messenger-at-arms, a police inspector, a superintendent and nine constables were prevented from entering Braes by a crowd which set about them with sticks and stones. In December the ironic outcome of the struggle was that Ben Lee, which had formerly been part of their holding, was leased to the crofters for grazing.

Meanwhile, the crofters of Glendale, in north-west Skye, were refusing to pay their rents. Four policemen and a messenger-at-arms who were despatched with summonses were set upon and beaten up. Thereafter several hundred crofters armed with sticks, scythes and graips marched to Dunvegan, to find the police had fled.

Early in 1883 the Government decided to take action. To

avoid military intervention five Glendale crofters were encouraged, and finally agreed, to stand trial in Edinburgh. On 15 March they were sentenced to two months' imprisonment and became known as the Glendale Martyrs. Meanwhile the Government was setting up a royal commission 'to inquire into the conditions of the crofters and cottars in the Highlands and Islands of Scotland'.On 8 May, under the chairmanship of Lord Napier, it began taking evidence at Braes. A crofter was defined as 'a small tenant of land with or without a lease, who finds in the cultivation of his holding a material portion of his occupation, earnings and sustenance and who pays rent directly to the proprietor'. The crofters slowly gained confidence in their ability to state their case, though they were still haunted by fear, as this extract from the Napier Commission report clearly shows:

Question: You will have the goodness to state what are the hardships and grievances, if any, of which the people whom you represent at this place complain.

Answer: I would wish that I should have an opportunity of saying a few words before I tell you that, and that is that I should have the assurance that I will not be evicted from my holding by the landlord or factor, as I have seen done already . . . I want the assurance that I will not be evicted, for I cannot bear evidence to the distress of my people without bearing evidence to the oppression and high-handedness of the landlord and his factor.

Assurances such as those asked for were reluctantly given. Mass meetings were held. In August crofters who were at Fraserburgh for the herring fishing resolved to form local branches of the Highland Land Law Reform Association. Circulars in Gaelic and English were issued. At last the crofters were organised and prepared to resort to terrorist tactics of destruction and intimidation. Still the unrest was felt most acutely in Skye. Time and again fences were pulled down, ricks fired, sheep driven from the grazings. In November 1884 the Government agreed to make troops available. A gunboat with 300 marines and a steamer as a mobile police barracks were provided and a force marched, fully armed, from Uig to Staffin. The crofters were amazed, and somewhat amused, at this dramatic show of strength.

In the following season, 1885-6, wool prices collapsed and landlords became anxious to settle with the crofters in order to get rents paid. A Crofters' Party had emerged at Westminster, which added to their worries. Finally, on 25 June 1886, Gladstone's government passed the Crofters' Holdings (Scotland) Act. This gave security of tenure to the crofter and compensation for improvements carried out by him, should he give up his tenancy. It allowed him to hand on the croft to a member of his family. It also set up a Crofters' Commission to fix fair rents, subject them to review, cancel arrears and administer the Act generally. The landlords were alarmed by the provisions of the Act, but the crofters were not satisfied. Still no attempt was made to make an adequate amount of land available. The Highlanders were a pastoral people, largely dependent on the rearing of cattle, and could not live with their land turned into sheep-runs and deer forests.

As unrest still smouldered the Highland Land Law Reform Association was reconstituted as the Highland Land League. With Salisbury's government in power and Balfour at the Scottish Office measures were tightened against rebellious tenants. In July 750 police and 250 marines were landed on the island of Tiree. Eight crofters were arrested and five imprisoned. In October Sheriff Ivory sent police and marines to serve summonses for arrears of rates on crofters in Glendale. The party was assaulted by the women while the men drove the cattle into the hills. By the following January the work of the Crofters' Commission was beginning to take effect. Rents were reduced and arrears cancelled.

Meanwhile, as herring prices had been falling, less money

was being made at fishing and demand for land again became acute. At Park, in Lewis, the people raided a deer forest and killed 100 deer. They made a makeshift camp, using sails as tents and roasting meat over fires in the open. Some sent carcasses home to their hungry families. A Government enquiry followed and troops were sent to quell the unrest. Not until two years later, when the fishing improved and the people were temporarily pacified, were the soldiers withdrawn.

At last, in 1897, more than ten years after the passing of the Crofters' Act, a serious attempt was made by the Unionist Government of the time to improve conditions for the crofting community. The Highlands Congested Districts Board was established in that year and funds were made available for construction of roads and bridges, for developing the tweed industry and fisheries, for fencing and draining, for spraying potatoes and for the establishment of a stock improvement programme, with the provision of bulls, tups and stallions. There is no doubt that these measures were of great importance in the development of the crofting areas generally. Yet still the people's craving was for land, for land that they could call their own.

In February 1906 raiders landed on the island of Vatersay, ferried over their sheep and cattle, and built houses for themselves. It was said in their defence that 'their grandparents and remoter ancestors had crofts on Vatersay at the very place where the raiders' huts were now set up—and though their grandparents had been evicted their descendants had never given up their claim. Throughout all the years their descendants down to this day have continued to bury their dead on Vatersay.' Two years later, in June 1908, ten of the raiders were imprisoned. In October of that year the Congested Districts Board bought Vatersay, after a tussle with the owner, and the raiders were given their holdings. It was clear that more had to be done before the crofters would feel that they were being fairly treated.

In 1911, after the passing of the Small Landholders (Scotland) Act, the Crofters' Commission became the

Scottish Land Court, to which appeal could be made in any case of injustice. The following year the Congested Districts Board became the Board of Agriculture for Scotland, which was to operate over the whole country and which had certain powers to settle people on land, the owners receiving compensation.

After the 1914-18 war there was more discontent and some raids took place. In December 1919 the Land Settlement (Scotland) Bill gave powers of compulsory purchase to the Board of Agriculture and provided loans to landholders. Still sporadic raids took place. Crofters who had been evicted, in 1850, from the fertile island of Raasay to the barren rocks of Rona, an islet to the north, returned to reclaim their original holdings. As a result, several people were imprisoned. Then, in 1922, the Board bought Raasay, but stipulated that no raiders be allowed to settle there.

By the late 1920s it could be said that the long struggle for land was over. Emigration overseas and to the towns and cities — with the attraction, for the younger people, of easier living — had reduced the numbers still determined to live by traditional pursuits.

Those who did stay found that their way of living had to fit more and more closely into that of the world at large, from which they were no longer isolated. During the Second World War cropping programmes and livestock rearing were regulated according to the needs of the nation at large. Grants and subsidies were forthcoming. As always in time of war a beleaguered island looked to its native providers.

With the coming of peace there was, inevitably, a slackening, but the wartime effort had shown what could be achieved by heavy agricultural machinery and chemical fertilisers in bringing marginal hill land into cultivation. People were now encouraged to stay on the land, but the amalgamation of small agricultural units into larger, more viable ones was inevitable, as living standards and expectations had risen. It had never been intended, of course, that the croft would provide a complete living. It was now more than ever essential that there should be ancillary occupations. In the post-war years these were increasingly in heavy construction work on roads and in hydroelectric schemes, in forestry and in tourism, as well as in the traditional fishing and weaving. Still the small unit was under threat.

In 1954 Professor Taylor of Aberdeen, who had been asked to form a commission of enquiry into crofting conditions, reported: 'The crofting system deserves to be maintained if only for the reason that it supports a free and independent way of life which in a civilisation predominantly urban and industrial in character is worth preserving for its own intrinsic quality.' These were brave and wise words. The following year a new Crofters' Commission was set up to administer the Crofters (Scotland) Act 1955. Under the terms of this Act the Commission has a duty to keep under review all matters relating to crofting, to see to the reletting of vacant crofts and the apportionment of common grazings, and to administer schemes of financial aid such as grants and loans to crofters. A statutory register of crofts is kept.

In 1961 certain amendments and additions were made to the Act of 1955. Flexibility was certainly needed as the pace of change in the world at large was increasing. It was becoming more clearly apparent that crofting must be linked to some form of industrial activity and that the non-agricultural use of the croft would be as important as the traditional crofting one.

The creation of the Highlands and Islands Development Board in 1966 gave impetus to this idea, as part of the function of this new body was to promote non-agricultural development in the crofting areas and thus to provide employment for the crofter and his family. Investment in the tourist industry was one way in which it was hoped this would be achieved.

The discovery of North Sea oil and the entry of Britain into the European Economic Community were matters of great concern to the crofting community and as such were closely studied by the Crofters' Commission and reported on to the Secretary of State. Then, on 10 June 1976, after nearly ten years of preparation and discussion and delay, the Crofting

Reform (Scotland) Act was passed. This was:

> An Act to confer new rights on crofters and cottars to acquire subjects tenanted or occupied by them; to confer rights on crofters to share in the value of land resumed by landlords or taken possession of compulsorily; to protect the interests of crofters and cottars from planning blight; to make further provision as to financial assistance for crofters, cottars and certain owner-occupiers of certain land; to make further provision as to the removal of land from crofting tenure; to amend the law with respect to common grazings; to extend the powers of the Scottish Land Court . . .

In other words, the crofter is given the right to purchase his house and garden ground for a nominal sum and to acquire the in-by land at a price calculated at fifteen times the rent. These measures encourage him to develop his land. At the same time the Commission keeps a watchful eye on proceedings and will not release land from crofting tenure if it is not in the interest of the community to do so.

So, over the last hundred years, the crofter has become a member of the complex social structure of the modern world. His tenure of the land has gradually become more secure. But crofting was always more than a system of land tenure. It was a way of living in a close-knit, warm community.

A Living from the Land

By the early nineteenth century, with the changes in land use which were taking place, the people were having to adapt to a new way of living. Sheep were being introduced on a large scale and the joint tenancies of land, worked on the run-rig system, were being replaced by the allocation of small individual holdings, each with a share in a common grazing on moor or hill. These crofts, or enclosed lands, were not, as we have seen, intended to provide all the means of subsistence for a family. They were meant to provide partial means of support while making their occupants available for work at kelping or fishing, or as hired hands on farms and estates. In a large, scattered area such as the Highlands from Argyll to Caithness and the Western and Northern Isles, ways of adapting to new conditions, of cultivating, stock-rearing, building houses, finding supplementary employment and so on were bound to vary, according to environment, climate and other factors. But between life on a croft in Barra and one in Shetland there were more similarities than differences.

With the long glens emptied, except for an imported shepherd here and there (Border names still crop up in remote parts of Wester Ross and Sutherland) the new settlements were mostly on barren upland and coastal strips. Families from the great inland straths of Sutherland who found themselves on a few windswept acres by a rocky shore must have had a hard time adjusting to this alien environment. Lives were lost as men put to sea in ramshackle boats or were swept from the rocks by wind and wave. In the west, where the people had never been far from the coast and where many had Viking origins, they yet were reluctant to depend on the sea as a provider. It had been their highway, of course, when there were no roads, their means of transporting people and things. The only access to some places cut off by hill and bog was by boat. But sallies were made at suitable times, in suitable weather. The people kept a healthy respect for this unpredictable element— water. They had been accustomed to catch fish at the head of a sea-loch by the simple device of a wall built across the narrows, behind which the fish were held as the tide went out, when they were easily taken in nets. Freshwater fish from loch and burn were quite readily available. Sea fishing on a commercial scale in the treacherous waters of the east, the west and the north demanded equipment beyond the reach of the crofter—sturdier boats, better gear of all kinds—and the building of docks and harbours. It was to be many years before these things were provided.

In the meantime, as the seafaring skills of the crofters developed, many would take work on the big boats sailing out of established ports and would be away for long stretches of time in the summer season. Though they usually managed to finish the ploughing before they left, much of the heavy field work of the croft—harrowing, grubbing, reaping and so on—had to be done by the women. They had, of course, long been in the habit of looking after the milk cow, the poultry and the few sheep and goats which were often kept. The woman was very much the key figure in the household. Many families lost their menfolk to the Army, as recruiting officers scoured the croft lands in the building of the Highland regiments. Agents of the press-gang were busy on behalf of the Navy, too. On occasion young fishermen were actually kidnapped at sea, forcibly taken from their boats, and in Orkney landowners were obliged to supply so many men for the Navy or pay a heavy fine.

The old communal pattern of life which had prevailed in the days of the joint tenancies still held good. Interdependence was absolute and especially so when the women were left on their own. The old, the sick and the children were looked after with unfailing devotion and at whatever cost in personal sacrifice. Households were often large. There was always room for a granny at the fire. She was usually able to spin or mend or rock a cradle. Old men could repair nets or tools. Even the bedridden had a place, making a focal point for concern, for suffering was accepted as part of the pattern. If some elderly relative preferred her independence, a small room would be built on to the end of the house or even a separate one-roomed dwelling would be put up nearby, so that she could be on her own, yet within reach of care should it be needed.

The households included, in winter, the cattle and hens, as well as dogs and cats. Often all the occupants came in by the same door, the cows turning one way and the people the other. The floor of the byre would be on a level lower than that of the kitchen, so that effluent was channelled off. Cows and humans generated heat to their mutual advantage in the coldest weather. Hens and cockerels roosted on the roof beams, in the smoke.

In spite of the crowded conditions, or perhaps because of them, there was a delicacy of behaviour between the sexes and between the generations, a dignity of bearing which was marvelled at by travellers of the time and which perhaps stemmed from the aristocratic structure of the old clan society.

Strangers were welcomed as they had always been. A very old Gaelic poem has these lines: 'I have put food in the eating place. I have put wine in the drinking place. . . For often, often, often comes the Christ in the stranger's guise. . . .'

No one admitted to poverty, though starvation might be only days away.

As rents in service or kind were commuted to money payments, cash had to be found for the landlord. Cash was also needed to buy meal, for the crofts were too small to grow enough for a family's needs. Paid employment was sought, not only by the men at the fishing, but also by the young women, who went off to the harvests on the big farms in the south. Travellers reported meeting bands of them coming home on foot over the hill passes, with bundles of trinkets and finery they had been tempted to buy with their earnings. The money economy which the chiefs had instigated a hundred years before was being adopted by all ranks of the clans.

Perhaps the greatest change which the new order of things brought to the people's lives was that they had virtually to give up their pastoral habits to become part-time agriculturalists. This must have been irksome to most of them, accustomed as they were to the free life of the herdsman. As the reindeer to the Lapp, so the cattle were to the Highlander. From very early times they had been the most highly prized asset a man could possess and, as such, they were often the object of raids by warring clans. Cattle-lifting was accepted as part of life. In some places watches were kept in glens through which the raiders passed.

The main festivals of the year were Beltane on the first day of May, when the cattle went out to the higher pastures, and Samhain on the first day of November, when they were brought into the shelter of the in-by land. At Samhain festival, fires were lit on the tops of hills and the cattle driven round them to keep away harm in the coming year.

During the sixteenth and seventeenth centuries large numbers of cattle were sent to the market at Crieff and, later on, at Falkirk, where they were bought by English dealers. There was an important trade in hide as well as in meat. The drovers' roads over the hills are still clearly seen in many parts as are the stances in flat, well-watered places where they rested the beasts and had them shod for passing over hard ground. Island cattle were swum over narrow sea passages, such as the one at Kylerhea, to join the mainland droves. Sometimes drovers stayed on in southern Scotland or in England doing seasonal work. It is said that their dogs could make the return journey on their own, stopping at places where they had been fed on the way south. Some drovers wore fine silver buttons on their coats to meet their expenses should they fall ill on the journey. It was certainly hard going, with oatmeal the chief sustenance, a plaid for a blanket and heather for a bed, but it provided a window on the world and a wealth of tales for the winter fireside.

Perhaps the main event of the year was the annual migration of the women and young people, with the cattle, to the upland pastures—the shielings. They usually set off in early summer and stayed till near harvest time. The men would go up a few days beforehand to repair the shieling huts. These were simple stone structures, thatched with turf or heather, with a central hearth and heather beds. Separate buildings were used to store dairying equipment—wooden pails, churns, cheese presses and so on. The cattle throve astonishingly on the sweet hill grass. The cows gave milk enough for the making of great quantities of butter and cheese. Sometimes the butter was preserved in kegs buried in the peat; much was consumed on the spot or sent down to the people in the crofts. For the women and girls and boys life at the shielings was quite idyllic. The womenfolk had their dairying to do and their spinning in the evenings, while the boys fished and hunted between their spells of herding. The

people left behind were carefree, too, with no marauding beasts to chase out of the unfenced crops. They could work in peace at building-repairs so that often the women would come home to a new-thatched house. All in all, it was a happy time and many songs were made on shieling life.

In the autumn the fattened cattle were sold off and the few kept for wintering were housed. Winter feed was only straw and a little meadow hay. By the following spring many beasts were so weakened that they had to be lifted from the byre. The milk cow, as the mainstay of the household, was given the best food, but even then she was only fit to calve every other year and gave scarcely two or three pints of milk a day. Lactation was short, according to modern standards, so goats' and ewes' milk would help to tide over part of the dry period. Occasionally, at a time of real need, in winter, a stirk which was not too weakly would be bled and the blood mixed with oatmeal to make what are still known as black puddings.

With the loss of their almost limitless grazings to sheep-farmers, the new-style crofters could keep only as many cattle as their small arable acreage and their 'souming' (allocation) of hill ground would allow. They elected constables to supervise the grazings and would fold the cattle to ensure control. In modern times cattle-raising makes much greater demands on the arable land, with the growing of turnips and grass for hay, so that most crofts now carry hill sheep, which are hardier feeders.

Goats were commonly kept on the early crofts. They could be expected to thrive reasonably well, even on the poorest of feeding. In Johnson and Boswell's tour of 1773 they met a family living on the shore of Loch Ness who kept sixty goats and had a pot on the fire 'with goats' flesh boiling'. Later on, when forest management became important, some landlords forbade goats because of the damage they did to the trees. Herds became feral and still roam the wilder upland straths, where they are welcome as they graze the rock ledges which are dangerous for sheep.

The old breed of Highland sheep were white or dun in

colour and had four or six horns. They were much smaller and less hardy than the sheep of modern times and were housed at night in winter and often tethered by day. Only a few were kept, for their fleece which was spun into fine yarn used in making the old 'hard' tartan, and for the ewes' milk which was made into cheese. Like the cows, they had low fertility, usually lambing only every other year.

The people were not long in adapting to the new circumstances and took readily enough to the pastoral activity of shepherding. They were well used to co-operative effort and enjoyed the gatherings for clipping, and for smearing with a mixture of tar and butter, which was the way of getting rid of maggots before dipping in a chemical wash was adopted. The wool of black-faced sheep was coarser than that of the old Highland breed but there was also a value in the meat. In 1817 a Wool Fair was established in Inverness for the sale of fleeces. It is still held, on the first Friday in July, but has now become mainly a horse market, for the fleeces are sent direct to the dealers.

As time went by the pastures became soured with overgrazing and began to deteriorate. Sheep eat out the fine grasses, allowing coarse growth to flourish. Disease became prevalent. Some of the shine came off sheep-farming on this outlandish scale.

With the Lowland flockmasters came the Border collies whose descendants work the sheep so magnificently today, and which, for intelligence and stamina, must have no equal anywhere in the world. Without them it would be quite impossible to handle large numbers of sheep. With the shepherds also came the fox hunters, with their brave little terriers which became known as 'cairns' since they often had to hunt the foxes out of rocky lairs.

Dogs had always figured largely in the life of the old Highlands. The great shaggy deerhounds were legendary beasts whose exploits were recorded in poem and story. They were as essential to the way of life of the hunter as the collie is to that of the shepherd today.

The other animal essential to the work of the land was the

horse. The traditional breed of Highland horse, the garron, was small, hardy and very sure-footed. He was ideally suited to work on croft land, where he carried loads of peat from the hill, or seaweed from the shore, and pulled light implements in the fields. He existed on scant feed, browsing happily on hill and moor. The many stretches of rough ground known as *caiplich*—the place of horses—show that these sturdy, useful little beasts were kept in large numbers. Later, with the coming of heavier implements, much bigger horses were needed and the garrons were crossed with heavier breeds of the Clydesdale type.

Pigs were not kept to any extent on the crofts. Indeed, in some places they were regarded as taboo. This may stem from the fact that the Picts do not appear to have been pork-eaters, though the Irish and the Norse certainly were.

Poultry were kept in fairly large numbers and generally had comfortable quarters roosting on the roof beams of the house. In Orkney small recesses were built into the walls of the kitchen where geese could nest in comfort. Like all the other livestock, hens and geese had to do a lot of foraging for themselves.

Cultivation. The thin, acid soil of the Highlands does not lend itself easily to cultivation. A crofter of the old school—wise, knowledgeable and skilled—was asked, not long before he lately died, what he considered had been the greatest help over the last century in improving the croft lands. He replied emphatically and without hesitation, 'the application of lime'. He said it was like a miracle how the fields shone green where lime was spread.

The people always knew they had hungry land and every means was used to feed it. Old roof thatch, impregnated with soot from the peat fire, was ploughed into the fields or spread as top dressing. Dung was carted from the midden and sea wrack from the shore. Even human excrement was applied, the men using the stable and the women the byre as latrines. The stalled beasts were bedded in turf or bracken and this material, soaked in urine, was of great value in building up humus.

Oats and bere had been grown for centuries. The oats were of the small, black variety, short-stalked, which stood up well to the wind. The bere was a kind of barley. The meal of both was used in baking and in a variety of dishes and drinks—bere bannocks are still made in Orkney today. But the continuous growing of grain crops meant that the land was never cleaned and fierce competition from weeds of all kinds led to stunted and uneven growth.

By the time the crofts were established potatoes had become important in the Highlander's diet. They took up less room than cereals and gave a good return even on poor ground. It was the people's increasing dependence on them which made the crop failure in 1846 so disastrous.

Wild grasses were howked out of every nook and corner, by river-banks and under scrub, sometimes with the bare hands, and dried as the weather permitted into some semblance of hay. The growing of sown hay and turnips, as part of a regular rotation, which had been practised in the eastern and central Highlands since the eighteenth century, was introduced gradually into the crofting areas. The cultivated grass was even more difficult to dry than were the wild varieties. Still today, in the west, one can see the hay hanging out, like washing, on the fences.

In the west and on the Islands, in places where the soil was exceptionally shallow, it was common practice to grow corn and potatoes in lazy-beds—*fiannegan*. These were long, narrow, raised beds made by turning two layers of turf one on top of the other, with a filling of seaweed in between. The raising meant good drainage of the plots. They were fashioned with the foot-plough—*cas chrom*, meaning crooked foot. This was a piece of naturally curved wood, about five feet long, fitted to a flat iron-tipped piece, with a peg where the foot was pressed as the worker, moving backwards, turned the clod. The *cas chrom* was used in the cultivation of small enclosed fields, as well as in making lazy-beds. Indeed, after the loss of the hill grazings for horses, many crofters

C

reverted to the *cas chrom*. It was reckoned that a man, working from January to April, could turn five acres. In Shetland, after the reorganisation of settlements into very small units in the eighteenth century, the ground would be turned by a delving team. They used short, straight spades, shod with iron, and worked in line abreast. This practice continued into modern times.

For breaking clods and lifting potatoes, the *croman*, an implement somewhat like a pick, was used. Once the ground was turned it had to be harrowed to make a fine tilth. On the lazy-beds this was done with a wooden-toothed implement, like a rake. The oldest harrows were made entirely of wood—frame and teeth—and were so light that they could be, and often were, pulled by the women. In the Western Isles the harrows were sometimes fastened to the horses' tails, which seems a barbarous custom, but was said to be a good way to break in a young horse.

Crop-shearing was originally done with the sickle, which meant that a fairly long stubble was left, as the effort of bending was extremely wearisome. The women doing the stooking would make rhythmic movements of the arms, keeping time by singing songs specially made for the work. Harvesting was a communal activity, though Wordsworth chanced upon a single Highland lass, reaping and singing and 'o'er the sickle bending'. By the early nineteenth century the scythe had replaced the sickle and fifty years later the mechanical horse-drawn reaper and then the binder came into use on the bigger crofts. There were many rites associated with the gathering-in of corn, most of them originating in pre-Christian times. The first sheaf cut was called the Maiden and was ornamented and put aside to be given to the horse setting out to plough the following spring. The last sheaf was known as the Old Woman—*cailleach*—and everyone tried to avoid having to cut it as it was considered unlucky. In some places, however, the *cailleach* was built into the top of the last stack and was thought to provide protection.

Late harvests meant damp grain and often it had to be

dried in kilns. In Caithness and Orkney kilns were often built onto the end of the barn where they could serve as an extra room for guests. After reaping, the grain was threshed and winnowed. In early crofting days the flail was used for threshing, several men working in unison in the airy threshing-barns. Winnowing, to rid the grain of husks, was done either on a piece of high ground or in the draught between the barn doors. The grain was tossed up so that the moving air would blow the chaff away. By the late nineteenth century mechanical fanners were in use on the bigger crofts. Graddaning, an extremely wasteful harvest practice, had been largely abandoned during the eighteenth century. It consisted of pulling up the grain crop by the roots, burning off the husk and beating off the grain. It was said that, in this way, the corn could be 'winnowed, ground and baked within an hour after reaping from the ground'.

For grinding the corn the earliest device was probably the

knocking-stone—*cnotag*—a large hollowed stone in which the grain was pounded with a wooden club. This method is still used in some African villages today. A primitive grinding implement dating from Roman times, yet still in use in remote places within living memory, was the rotary quern. It consisted of two flat round stones with a hole in the middle of the upper one through which the grain was fed. Two smaller holes in the rim of the upper stone held pegs which were gripped by the two operators, usually women, who squatted on the ground and turned the stone. The work could be done by a single operator.

Small horizontal mills were set up on lades channelled off streams in hilly country. Many may still be seen in Shetland today. They were in common use until the building of vertical mills in the fifteenth and sixteenth centuries. Some lairds regarded these as sources of profit and forbade the use of hand-mills, compelling tenants to use the common mill and to contribute a portion of the meal as fee, to undertake maintenance of the mill, the dam and the lade and to help transport new millstones when needed.

Another kind of small mill was used in some places in the eighteenth and nineteenth centuries—a whin-mill for crushing shoots of gorse to provide a supplement of fodder for cattle and horses. It was reckoned that an acre of whins could keep six horses for four months and the whins might even be specially sown. They could also be threshed out with the flail or bruised in the knocking-stone.

Peat. To feed the family and the animals on which it depended was the aim of all the year's work of ploughing, sowing, reaping, and herding. To provide winter warmth yet another activity was, and still is, engaged in—peat-cutting. Wood was scarce in many parts of the crofting areas. Peat was plentiful in most places and the right to cut it was an essential part of crofting tenure. The work fitted well enough into the pattern of the year's husbandry. It was a communal activity and was enjoyed as a chance for scattered neighbours to meet and exchange news and gossip. When the fields were worked, the crops sown and the cattle out on the new grass, the people would set off to the peat-banks on the hill. With another win-ter survived, the larks sing-ing and the air blowing sweet off the moor, there was a feel of holiday about the outing. Baskets of food would be loaded, along with the peat-knives, onto the horses' backs, and an early start made to the long day.

The work is hard. The elderly or infirm have their winter fuel won for them by the young and strong. First the bank is prepared with the flaughter spade—*cabar lar*. This implement has a long, curved shaft, a crossbar at the top and an iron blade which is pushed along the ground, skimming off surface growth. Then, with the peat-knife, or peat-spade, a straight-shafted implement with a flanged blade, the soft peat is cut out in blocks. This is work for the men, while the women and children spread the slabs to dry. After a morning's labour everyone relaxes over a meal of bannocks and cheese, perhaps baked potatoes, with a drink of buttermilk or tea brewed on a fire of heather roots. The children still have energy to scamper happily about, pelting each other with lumps of peat and laughing out of blackened faces.

In reasonably good weather the blocks can be built immediately into small stooks of three to five, with one across the top. After a week or two they are piled in larger heaps and in late summer they are barrowed, carted or tractor-driven home and made into stacks near the house. Today, in Lewis and Caithness, one can see peat-stacks which dwarf the dwellings. Peat was such an essential commodity, before other means of providing heat were available, that, in some of the western Islands where there was none to be had, the people would cut it on another island and bring it home by the boatload.

The quality of peat varies from region to region. The brown, fibrous kind makes poorer burning than the black, dense type. When thoroughly dry and hard, good peat gives a fine, glowing heat. In some houses in older times, the fire never went out, even in two hundred years. It would be smoored in the evening, that is covered over with ash, and blown into life in the morning. Catrine MacPharlan, a crofter's wife in Barra, gave this smooring blessing to Alexander Carmichael when he was collecting Gaelic poems and songs about a hundred years ago:

> I will smoor the hearth
> As Mary would smoor;
> The encompassment of Bride and of Mary,
> On the fire and on the floor,
>   And on the household all.

Fire, like water, was an element to be respected.

Skills for Living

*T*he House. For people living a hard outdoor life and working long hours, often in harsh conditions, a house was essentially a refuge from the elements, a place where shelter and warmth could be found. Houses on the early crofting settlements were built of whatever materials were readily available, by people working together, as was the custom. It is said that a simple dwelling for a newly married couple could be put up in a day. House types varied according to the materials and to the weather conditions prevailing. In Lewis, as a protection against Atlantic gales, the end walls were rounded and the thatched roofs low and domed, with the thatch held down by weighted ropes. On the mainland square gables were preferred. Sometimes turf was used for walling, more often stone. The walls might be six feet thick and double, with earth between the layers. To step out of a raging storm into the quiet of such a house gives an incredibly reassuring feeling of security and comfort. The roof was made of couples, pairs of tree trunks standing against the inner wall, or on the floor of the house, with their tops tied or pegged together. The roof tree .was placed along the tops of the couples. Beside them were laid slender poles, close together, and on the poles a layer of sods and then of thatch, made of heather, rushes or straw. In Orkney, twisted straw, called 'simmons', was laid as a lining below the thatch. In Caithness, flagstones were used in roofing. To this day one sees them serving also as fencing material, as partitions in byres, even as foundations for cattle grids. Windows, if there were any, were very small, sometimes with wooden shutters, and the door was low.

Sometimes a partition that did not reach the roof separated off the cattle's byre. The partition walls were often of willow or hazel wands, infilled with straw and clay. A hole in the roof let out most of the smoke from the fire, but some of it escaped through the thatch so that, from outside, the whole roof would appear to be smouldering. Much of it lingered in the room, too, and the occupants sat on low chairs or stools so as to be below the pall.

In later houses the fire would be built against a stone backing on a partition wall and would have a hanging lum, a canopy made of timber and clay to draw the smoke out through a chimney. Later still, the fireplace would be at the gable wall, with a built-in flue. Pots would be hung from an iron chain—*slabhraidh*—fixed to a crosspiece in the roof or chimney. These chains were blacksmith-made and were a kind of status symbol, as iron was expensive and the possession of a fine chain was a sign of affluence. With the gable chimney a swee was used. This was an iron bar fixed to the side of the fireplace, with an arm which could swing free, holding the pot either over the fire or over the hearth. A brander, a kind of iron rack, was placed over the fire for grilling fish. Flat girdles were used for making scones and oatcakes and baking could be done in a pot, with a burning peat placed on the lid.

The Diet. With oatmeal, milk and eggs the main items of food, cooking was limited in scope yet, with the addition of potatoes and fresh fish — or salt fish when the salt tax did not bear too hard — and the occasional dish of meat or game, it was a healthy enough diet and a surprising number of variations could be achieved. One was an early type of milk-shake. A short stick with a circle of cow's hair fixed on a small frame at the end, called a fro-stick — *loineid beag* — was used to whisk a dish of milk to a froth. This was called broken milk and was served with a sprinkling of oatmeal. Boswell, in the famous *Tour*, records: 'At Auchnashiel we sat down on a green turf seat at the end of a house; they brought us out two wooden dishes of milk, which we tasted. One of them was frothed like a syllabub. I saw a woman preparing it with such a stick as is used for chocolate, and in the same manner.' A special treat was beestings — the first milk from a newly calved cow, which was flavoured with sugar and left to set to a custard-like consistency. Buttermilk was enjoyed as a refreshing drink.

The rarer additions to the diet varied from place to place. In the hill areas a 'braxy' ewe would occasionally provide a mutton stew. Gulls' eggs were collected in many parts. In the Northern Isles geese were kept for their meat and feathers. The people of Ness, in the north of Lewis, went to Sula Sgeir to catch gannets for salting. The St Kildans depended almost entirely on harvesting sea birds and their eggs. The men would perform incredibly dangerous feats to secure their prey, dangling on ropes over the cliffs, where they took gannets, puffins and fulmar.

All in all, the people's fare was scanty, though wholesome

enough. A typical day's intake, excluding any of the occasional additions, over most of the crofting areas might have been something like this:

Breakfast: Gruel and bread or, brose (raw oatmeal moistened with water) and milk

Dinner: Potatoes and milk

Supper: Potatoes, gruel of kale. In summer, porridge and milk, with bread.

'Bread' was bannocks of oatmeal. For a special treat they would be coated with a batter of eggs, milk and butter before toasting at the fire. The only vegetable grown, apart from potatoes, seems to have been kale. But use was made of seaweeds, where they were available, such as dulse and carrageen. They were washed and dried, then boiled in milk and flavoured and were considered a delicacy. Nettle soup was commonly made and charlock and silverweed were eaten. These items helped to give some balance to the diet.

Furnishings. The box-bed, sometimes quite an elaborate affair, with panelled doors, was the usual sleeping-place of the family. It was a most useful item of furniture, serving as a room-divider, providing a bunk-like sleeping-space for one or more children on the top and storage underneath. The dresser was simply a sort of side-table with shelves and a plate-rack attached, introduced once wooden vessels had been superseded by pottery in the course of the nineteenth century. Cupboards for holding foodstuffs sometimes had sides made of wickerwork to keep the contents aired and fresh.

In the days of the central hearth, when the family sat, literally, round the fire, and as near to it as possible on winter nights, tables do not appear to have been used for eating. A bowl or plate on the knee was usual. Some of the low chairs were quite stylishly made, in imitation of the fashions prevailing in grander houses of the time. Along one wall was often a seise, or settle, usually joiner-made and sometimes with the seat forming a blanket-box.

For lighting, fish oil was used in the cruisie-lamps, with peeled rushes as wicks. As the smell was strong, they were usually hung near the fire so that the stench would mingle with the smoke. In inland districts fir candles were made from pine wood that had been buried in the peat moss. Later, candles of mutton fat were cast in tin moulds. The fire itself gave a certain amount of light and the people of the old crofts must have spent many a winter's evening spinning, carding and mending nets with only the peat-glow to guide them.

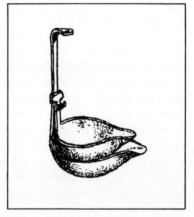

Utensils such as potato-mashers, ladles, spurtles for stirring porridge, and beetles for pounding dirt out of clothes on the river-bank were made of wood, often at home, simply by whittling. Spoons were sometimes of horn, shaped in a mould.

The Crafts. Early crofters, especially those in the more isolated districts, had perforce to be Jacks-of-all-trades. They were adept at crafting the materials they found to hand. Rope, for instance, was made from straw, heather, rushes or horsehair. It could be fashioned by hand, simply by two people standing at a distance from each other and twisting the strands, or by means of an implement called a 'thrawcrook', a hook with a handle. Pot-scrubbers were made from dried heather twigs, tightly bunched and bound with thread to form a handle. Baskets were fashioned for many purposes—as creels for carrying peats or seaweed, as panniers for ponies, as containers for potatoes or fish bait. Basket bodies were sometimes built onto sledges or slipes for carrying loads of dung. Willow or hazel wands or closely woven bent grass were the materials used.

A shoemaker was to be found in every community and the repairing of boots and shoes was carried on in every house. Rivelins, a primitive kind of footgear made of untanned calfskin worn hairy side out and held together by laces, were worn till lately in some parts of Caithness and Orkney. They gave a firm foothold on slippery rocks.

The crafts most closely associated with the women are dyeing, spinning and weaving wool. In the early nineteenth century an attempt was made, in parts of the eastern and northern Highlands, to provide employment for women in making linen yarn from flax, but this was not a fruitful enterprise as there was work enough for those women who wanted it in net-making for the herring industry and it was soon found that flax-spinning could be done more profitably by machines in the south.

Wool-spinning was traditionally done with the spindle. A woman would wind a piece of fleece round a length of wood—the distaff—which she held in the crook of her left arm, work it into a thread, twist it and feed it onto a dangling, weighted piece of wood—the spindle. It was a lengthy process, but at least the spinner could carry it out while doing some other job, such as herding cattle or even bringing creel-loads of peat from the moor. The spinning-wheel as we know it today was only introduced during the nineteenth century. Its predecessor was the muckle wheel, a large wheel connected to a spindle by a band. It was turned by hand, the operator pulling out and twisting the thread, moving backwards as she did so, then reversing the movement, so that the thread was spun. This, too, was laborious and meant that the woman walked miles in the course of a day. The more recent Saxony wheel is worked by a treadle. Once she has acquired the knack a woman can spin much greater quantities of yarn with this device and can sit at her work by the fire or out in the sun on a summer's day, with a daughter beside her teasing out the wool into a fluffy roll with a pair of carders.

In places where there was a nearby mill or a weaver the yarn would be sent there to be made up into blankets or cloth.

In the Islands much weaving was done at home. When the web was taken from the loom it had to be further processed by shrinking. This was a communal activity, known as waulking the cloth. About a dozen neighbours would take part, sitting on the ground or on opposite sides of a trestle table. The cloth, which had been soaking in urine, was passed round sun-wise, the women thumping it rhythmically as they sang, slowly at first and gradually working up to fever pitch. This was an all-female activity and many of the songs poked fun at men. Woe betide any unfortunate male who happened to appear during the proceeding! Finally, the cloth was rolled, stretched, rolled again and a blessing put on it. As with all communal activities a lot of fun ensued, teasing and laughter, and there would be food and drink for everyone before the journey home.

What gave cloth woven in the Highlands its special beauty was the skill of the women in finding and using the dye plants which produced the colours in the wool. Dyeing was usually done in the open air. In a large iron pot would be placed layers of wool and the dye plant, with a sprinkling of

mordant to fix the colour and a filling of water. On a fire of heather roots and peat the mixture was boiled up and stirred, till the worker judged the colour was as she wished. Many plants were used in the dyeing process. Lichens gave various shades of brown, lady's bedstraw gave red, black came from alder or the roots of tormentil, yellow from birch leaves or heather.

During the time of distress following the failure of the potato crop in the mid-nineteenth century some landowners and their ladies encouraged the making of cloth. It had come to be known as 'tweed', particularly in the island of Harris, where lady Dunmore helped to set up looms for the crofters. The people's natural skill, developed over the years, their eye for colour and knowledge of dyes made the enterprise a success. The cloth was sold initially to the well-to-do people who were coming about the Highlands in the wake of the Victorian court. Gradually the demand for it spread until it became, and still is, a famous export with an association— the Harris Tweed Association—protecting its interests and maintaining standards.

The knitting of stockings was also done, on a piecework basis, the wool being supplied by the organisers of the scheme. The women would take their knitting with them when herding or going to and from the peat-banks or the shore with their loads of peat and seaweed. In Shetland the wool of the native sheep was soft and more suitable for knitting than for weaving. There had been a demand for knitted stockings by Dutch fishermen who visited the islands as early as the seventeenth century. Later, the intricate Scandinavian patterns evolved on Fair Isle were introduced all over Shetland and knitting developed into an important industry which did more than pay the crofter's rent.

Clothing. The people themselves wore plain homespun clothing. For the women this consisted generally of a long skirt of dark cloth which could be bunched at the back, like a bustle, to make a support for the creels they so often carried. They also wore blouses, with a shawl or plaid in winter. Stockings, for men and women, were made of cloth. Sometimes women wore soleless stockings, looped over the toe, called 'moggans'. On her wedding morning the young bride first wore her mutch, to show her new estate, and thereafter she took great pride in having a spotless white headpiece always ready to put on. Special goffering irons were made for smoothing the frills.

After 1747, when the Disarming Act forbade wearing the kilt, as well as carrying weapons, men were obliged to abandon their native form of dress. The Act was repealed in 1782 but by then many had taken to wearing trousers of drab cloth. For fishermen the kilt was not suitable garb in any case. By the eighteenth century people who were earning a little from occupations ancillary to the croft tended to buy factory-made cloth or to have their clothes made by tailors.

As for tartan, the word itself is popularly thought to derive from the French *tiretaine*, which means a kind of material, not a colour. It is certain that the Highland people did weave checked fabrics. This would seem to tie in with the complex forms of their other artistic expressions — the interlaced patterns in Celtic design, the intricate verse forms and pipe tunes. How each clan came to be associated with a particular sett is not clear, but with the raising of the Highland regiments there was much professional weaving of tartan for the men and some regimental tartans seem to have become associated with particular clans. The arrival of the Victorian court in the Highlands created a vogue for tartan which has now spread worldwide.

The Still. The ploy that was engaged in exclusively by the men of the crofts was whisky distilling. Illicit it may have been but nevertheless it was practised in nearly every part of the Highlands. It was certainly a skilled affair and the risk involved seems to have been an added attraction. Inventing ways to outwit the gaugers, or excisemen, became almost a form of sport. It also had its economic necessity. When times were hard and rents rising it was certainly tempting to make a product with a ready sale.

The work was carried on in small, rough and ready bothies in secluded spots in woodland or among rocks on a nearly smokeless fire of dry juniper and heather the brew could be made in broad daylight. Sometimes the kitchen fire was used at night. Overindulgence in the product occasionally led to tragedy. A man seeking to douse some despair would stumble on the narrow path from a hillside

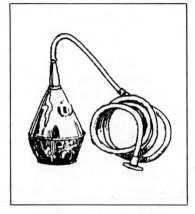

bothy and crash to his death in a ravine. Another might be aroused to fury and draw a knife on a fellow smuggler.

But there are many good tales of outwitting excisemen, of kegs of whisky hidden in the voluminous folds of chairbound granny's long skirt or in the winding-sheet of a faked corpse laid out on the table. Sometimes, in desperation when the gaugers were hot on the trail, pot, worm and cask would be flung into a nearby bog or lochan, to be retrieved later.

Substantial bribes were offered to the people to inform on smugglers, but it is not recorded that any were accepted — unless by arrangement, for the purchase of new equipment.

In 1823 vigorous measures were adopted to stamp out smuggling but seventy years on gear was still being seized.

The other traditional Highland brew was ale, made from barley or heather. It is still the favoured drink in Orkney, where most houses have a cask or two bubbling in the kitchen. By the mid-nineteenth century tea had become the universally accepted beverage. To this day the teapot is hardly ever empty and one is always welcomed with a *strupach*, a cup of hot-and-strong.

The Craftsmen. Though every crofter was, of necessity, skilled in many crafts, as was his wife, yet there were certain jobs essential to the maintenance of life in a rural community which required some specialised training and were more or less full-time occupations. Perhaps the most important of these was the job of blacksmith. The forging of iron is one of the oldest crafts in the world. In the Highlands it had its own mystique, as iron was considered to have magical properties. Watching a blacksmith at work today one can still catch a glimpse of the magic as the molten metal, first red, then white-hot, is worked and shaped. In the early crofting settlements the blacksmith's work consisted mainly of making tools such as sickles, the cutting ends of peat-knives and *cas chroms* and household equipment—pots, girdles, fire-chains and swees. In Jura, in the 1880s, the tenants of one clachan paid the smith fifteen shillings a year for his work and it was said that 'the crofters must each provide his own fuel, blow the bellows and work the forehammer'.[1] As roads improved to the point where they could carry carts, wheelwrights and carpenters set up as near as possible to the smithy. For those who could afford them, wheeled vehicles took the place of home-made slipes and sledges.

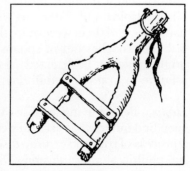

[1] John Mercer: *Hebridean Islands—Colonsay, Gigha, Jura* (Blackie, 1974).

Other craftsmen who were supported, at least in part, by the community were joiners, masons and tailors. The joiners made wooden churns, cheese presses, pails and other staved vessels as well as furniture. As house styles became a little more elaborate masons were employed in dressing stone. They also made headstones. In more isolated places tailors stayed in the customer's home while working on their jobs and were fed as well as paid. Their arrival would be welcome, for they brought news and gossip and many would contribute song and story to the evening gathering. There were more tailors about than one would imagine, one reason being, no doubt, that the people were adept at making good cloth. Another may have been that the Celt has always been fond of dressing well.

In coastal areas boat-builders were obviously in great demand. Their skills were highly specialised and they would receive appropriate rewards for their work. With the development of fishing, coopers were also needed for making herring barrels. This was another highly skilled job requiring sophisticated tools.

Many of these artisans who kept the settlements going were the descendants of cottars, the landless people who lived on the edge of the former run-rig farms and worked for their keep. The tinkers, some of whose forebears had been 'out in the '45'—that is, had fought in the Jacobite rebellion of 1745 — and had taken to the heather and never returned to a settled life, supplied useful items to the crofting community. These included horn spoons, heather pot-scrubbers, birch besoms and, later on, wooden clothes pegs and tin pans. Some of them were quite skilled silversmiths and could fashion brooches out of spoons melted down so that their origin could not be detected. Many could scrape a tune from a fiddle to brighten a dull day.

Healing. People living in close contact with natural resources soon find out to what uses they can be put. It must have been a process of trial and error to discover how ills could be cured by poultices and infusions. Still in little croft gardens camomile grows in profusion, though no one now infuses the florets to help headaches and indigestion. Sloe jelly is seldom made, for it is quicker to get a bottle of cough mixture on prescription. Foxgloves brought sleep, plantain soothed sores, marsh trefoil cured colic, primroses were pounded with butter to make a healing ointment.

From very early times there was a belief in magical cures and traces of this still linger. Water and fire were the great purifiers. The veneration of spring water was widespread and many wells were said to have curative properties. To this day an old person in hospital welcomes most gladly the gift of a bottle of water straight from the spring—water that has not come through pipe or tap.

Fire worship must have been behind the origin of the 'need fire', the practice of extinguishing the fire in every house, kindling a fresh one by rubbing together dry sticks, and then relighting the domestic fires. This was done in times of dire emergency or to avert calamity, such as plague on cattle or men.

One common form of cure, still practised here and there, was the application of silvered water. This is water taken from a place where 'the dead and the living passed', which meant a ford or a bridge on the way to a graveyard. A silver coin was dropped into the water before it was administered.

Charm stones were commonly used. They were dipped into drinking-water or worn hanging round the neck. Shock treatment, such as the sudden application of heat from molten iron or the flinging of a hysterical patient into cold water, was sometimes resorted to in emergency.

It was recommended that warts should be licked before. breakfast! For toothache lesser spearwort was to be laid at the base of the tooth. Bloodletting was a common practice. Smallpox was contracted deliberately by borrowing the underwear and blankets of those who had suffered or died from it. The only treatment given, as for measles, was a dose of whisky and sulphur. Tuberculosis and diphtheria were dreaded scourges on the crofts until well into the twentieth century. The early deaths recorded on gravestones are evidence of this and school records show the people's fear of infection. A typical Log Book entry reads: 'The people would not allow their children back to school till the premises had been disinfected' (by burning sulphur candles).

In the days when the Lords of the Isles dominated the civilisation of the Gaels there were learned physicians in the land. The Beatons of Islay were the most famous. They started a tradition of medical learning which died out only in the general stifling of Gaelic culture in the seventeenth and eighteenth centuries. Today doctors are still highly regarded in crofting communities and may serve the people with unfailing devotion, often, in winter storms, at great risk to their personal safety. I have lately heard of one who, since the recent severe winters has, at his own expense, invested in a snowmobile so that he can reach his patients quickly when they need him most.

The Lively Minds

To those whose lives depend directly on the forces of the natural world, on sun and storm, frost and drought, what is known as a religious outlook comes quite naturally. They have only to observe and to wonder, and worship, tinged with a desire to placate, follows. The early missionaries of the Celtic church wisely grafted their teaching on to forms already understood. Venerated wells were given the names of holy men—St Ninian or St Columba. As time went on the Christian faith itself took new forms and ways of worship were changed, but the people's need to find a meaning for life, to link it fore and aft to something that could be grasped by the mind and the heart, did not diminish.

In the earliest Christian times each simple act of everyday life had an appropriate prayer or blessing. Alexander Carmichael, in the late nineteenth century, collected many of these in his journeys through the Highlands. There was a 'Blessing of the kindling' for the morning as there was a 'Smooring blessing' for the evening, a 'Sleep prayer', a 'Consecration of the seed', a 'Milking blessing', a 'Journey blessing', a 'Rune before prayer', such as the one which starts:

I am bending my knee
In the eye of the Father who created me,
In the eye of the Son who purchased me,
In the eye of the Spirit who cleansed me,
　　In friendship and affection. . . .

In a note to this 'Solitary prayer' Carmichael says, 'From
Ann MacDonald, crofter's daughter, Lochaber. Old people
in the Isles sing this or some other short hymn before prayer.
They generally retire to a closet, or an outhouse, to the lee of
a knoll, or to the shelter of a dell, that they may not be seen or
heard of men. I have known men and women of eighty,
ninety and a hundred years of age continue the practice of
their lives in going from one to two miles to the seashore to
join their voices with the voicing of the waves and their
praises with the praises of the ceaseless sea.'

The priest and later the minister was, and still is, like the
doctor, a most influential member of a crofting community.
There is no doubt that, at the time of the clearances, the
religious teaching of the time had a great effect on morale. A
few ministers, such as Donald Sage in Sutherland, came out
on the side of the people. Most supported the landowners
and preached the doctrine that eviction was a just
punishment for past wickedness.

With their lives moving to the rhythm of the changing
seasons it came to people naturally to celebrate the big
events in the calendar—Beltane, pasturing the herds and
sowing the seed in spring; and Samhain, the return of the
herds to shelter and harvesting of crops in autumn. The
mingling of Christian and pre-Christian belief is shown in
this extract from 'The Beltane Blessing', in Carmichael's
collection:

> Bless, O Threefold true and bountiful,
> Myself, my spouse, and my children,
> My tender children and their beloved mother at their head.
> On the fragrant plain, on the gay mountain sheiling,
> On the fragrant plain, on the gay mountain sheiling.
>
> Everything within my dwelling or in my possession,
> All kine and crops, all flocks and corn,
> From Hallow Eve to Beltane Eve,
> With goodly progress and gentle blessing,
> From sea to sea, and every river mouth,
> From wave to wave, and base of waterfall. . . .

At Beltane, special bannocks were baked. Girls would wash their faces in the dew at dawn in the hope of acquiring beauty.

At Samhain household fires were rekindled with flame from bonfires on the hill. Samhain became All Saints' Day and the evening before—Hallowe'en—became the time for rites of a secular kind. Witches and warlocks were said to be abroad that night and people went about in disguise. Many tricks were played on the unwary—letting loose a styed pig being fattened for Christmas, blocking windows with sods or throwing peats down chimneys. It was also a time for divination rites. Girls quite seriously believed that if they ate enough salt herring to make them thirsty their future husbands would appear in their dreams, offering a drink. A kale stalk pulled at dusk would foretell the stature of the partner-to-be. There were also the well-known games of dooking for apples in a tub of water and snatching mouthfuls of treacle scones hung on a rope.

Christmas, since the Reformation, had not been observed on any great scale until quite recently. It is not long since it was kept according to the old calendar, on what is now Twelfth Night. New Year's Eve, Hogmanay, in Gaelic *a Challuinn,* is a time of great celebration. Until lately, rituals were performed which must have been survivals from very ancient times. In Lewis bands of young men, each with a leader draped in a sheepskin or cow hide, would go into the houses and walk clockwise round the fire, while everyone present beat the skin with a stick. The housewife would be expected to give the youths bannocks and other food and, if she did so, she received a blessing on her house. Today the observances are simpler. As midnight strikes guns are fired, to ward off evil spirits. Then people set out to first foot their neighbours, carrying a bottle of whisky and a baking of bannocks as a wish for prosperity to the household.

On New Year's Day, in older times, a great game of shinty would be played. Two rival townships or parishes would take sides, with no restriction on numbers, and play would range far and wide, over fields and moors until darkness brought it to an end, when often a fight would follow, with all the men of the countryside involved. Shinty is still played, with great skill and enthusiasm, though now rules have been evolved and a side is restricted to eleven members.

The Highland Games, which are now held every summer in many places, were originally trials of strength between rivals in a community. Tossing the caber—pitching a tree trunk to make it somersault—may have originated in the tossing of felled timber out of a wood. Casting the stone and hurling the hammer are feats recorded in very old folk tales. Latterly the men would practise these skills while waiting at the forge for the smith to complete some job for them. The introduction of piping and dancing into the contests is of much more recent date.

Beltane, Samhain and the mid-winter festivities of Christmas and New Year, at the time of the winter solstice, could all be said to be festivals of the sun. Great respect was also paid to the moon. Many an old person will still bow to the first sliver of moon she or he glimpses in a clear sky. Seed was sown in a waxing moon, peat was dug on the wane.

Church festivals which lingered on after they were officially discouraged at the Reformation were Candlemas (2 February), Easter, St John's Mass (24 June)—this particularly in Orkney when purifying fires were again lit on the hills—and St Michael's Day (29 September) which was an occasion for holding great horse races in the Western Isles.

There were certain beliefs and habits connected with days of the week. Tuesday was considered an auspicious day for a wedding. Thursday, St Columba's day, was the best one for making a start at anything. A cowherd in South Uist gave Carmichael a poem about this. It runs:

> Thursday of Columba benign,
> Day to send sheep on prosperity,
> Day to send cow on calf,
> Day to put the web in the warp.
>
> Day to put coracle on the brine,
> Day to place the staff to the flag,

Day to bear, day to die,
Day to hunt the heights.

Day to put horses in harness,
Day to send herds to pasture,
Day to make prayer efficacious,
Day of my beloved, the Thursday,
 Day of my beloved, the Thursday.

Friday was a day to plant and sow. It was unlucky to spin on a Saturday night. Sunday was the day to wash and put on clean clothes.

These daily and seasonal observances gave a shape to living and cast an aura of ceremonial over even the most tedious tasks. It was, I think, the sense of wholeness, of body, mind and spirit all being involved in day-to-day activities and of the individual being an essential part of the widening units of family and community, all working closely with the natural world, that gave meaning and purpose to the people's lives and helped them to survive almost insuperable difficulties.

Travellers in the Highlands at the time of the establishment of the crofts nearly all recorded their amazement at the distinguished manners and bearing of people living often in conditions of extreme poverty. There can be no doubt that this stemmed partly from their code of life which toughened moral fibre and also from their heritage as descendants of the old aristocratic clan society. Many could recount their whole line of ancestry back to far-off times, as still today the older people can.

The forms of artistic expression at which the people had always excelled were those of story-telling, poetry, music, song and dance. The long dark evenings of winter were a time to look forward to when they were spent with friends who could repeat the tales of long ago, or improvise a satire on the spur of the moment. Mrs Grant, in her *Letters from the Mountains*, said of Speyside, 'In every cottage there is a musician and in every hamlet a poet.'

The old epic tales of Finn MacCoul and the Feinne, the

E

soldiers of fortune who became an order of chivalry in the third and fourth centuries and whose exploits took them all over Ireland and Scotland and into Europe, were handed down through the ages and constantly added to. Deirdre, Grainne and Cuchulain had become household names. When clan society flourished the chiefs had bards among their following, highly skilled professional poets who recorded events and commented on people and affairs in polished verse. In the later seventeenth and eighteenth centuries poetry was composed by people of all walks of life. Many could neither read nor write and unfortunately much of their work has not been recorded, but their gifts were handed on. Still today there are men and women putting their thoughts and feelings into metric form who would die of embarrassment should anyone think of publishing their compositions for a readership of strangers. For their familiar audience of relatives and friends they would gladly recite their reflections on the beauty of the landscape or their satirical comments on an unpopular figure in the community.

Closely allied to poetry is song and it is, perhaps, in singing that the people of the Highlands express themselves most wholeheartedly. In the Hebrides every common task had its accompaniment in song. There were milking songs, spinning songs, rowing songs, songs for reaping, for weaving and shrinking the cloth. Some of the most beautiful were lullabies and laments, but there were also happy love songs and teasing, satirical songs, songs for every mood and occasion. Mouth-music, a kind of rhythmic humming, was used as an accompaniment for dancing.

The bagpipe was a martial instrument when the chiefs had their hereditary pipers. With the ceasing of clan warfare much highly stylised music was composed for the pipes. Schools of piping were set up, the most famous being that of the MacCrimmons of Skye. The harp—*clàrsach*—was not much played after the end of the seventeenth century when the fiddle came into use. In Strathspey and in Shetland this became a very popular instrument and has remained so. In the nineteenth century the accordion, commonly called 'the box', was adopted as a very suitable accompaniment to reels and quick dances. Originally the dance was probably an incitement to battle and performed only by men, but as fighting became less common everyone found it an excellent way to express joy or to shake off sorrow.

In 1891 a society called *An Comunn Gaidhealach* was formed. Its purpose is to encourage the study and advancement of Gaelic culture. Every October a Mod is held under its aegis. This is a series of competitions, spread over a week, in Gaelic choral and solo singing, verse-speaking, piping and fiddle playing. On the final day, a Bard is crowned, should his composition come up to the required standard. These competitions draw a highly appreciative audience, critical because well-informed, and have done much to maintain traditions.

Long before the official Mod was ever thought of the people had been holding their own gatherings in the winter evenings. These were the *ceilidhs*. Usually one particular house was a favoured one as a meeting place and was known as a *ceilidh* house. Neighbours would gather as darkness fell, each one bringing a small contribution—milk or bannock, cheese or peat. The women would often work at their knitting or spinning, the men would slowly fill their pipes and exchange comments on the weather and items of local or national news. The *Fear an Tigh*—the man of the house— would tell a story, then call for a song, then another, a ghost tale, a set of riddles, or an impromptu satire on a recent happening. When the company had worked up a thirst there would be tea and bannocks and a dram or two. If there was a fiddler itching to play the younger ones would dance and not till the small hours would the company disperse, for rising was later in the winter mornings. There would be much leave-taking as neighbours groped their way off in the dark, with a glowing peat for a torch and cries of 'Haste ye back!', before the fire was finally smoored and the hosts could retreat to bed.

It was these gatherings that put heart into everyone and

helped them through the worst of winters. Secure in their shared acceptance of the ways of their world, they could even cope with the fear that still lingered at the back of many minds and was perhaps revived by the hearing of a tale at a *ceilidh*, fear of the supernatural. To include this element in one's universe was really only an extension of the quest for wholeness. There had to be an 'unchancy' (ill-omened) factor somewhere. It might take the form of the kelpie, the *each uisge* or water horse, who lured the unwary into his kingdom under the waves. Still today in an upland strath near Inverness the older people will not willingly pass by a certain loch after dark. In Orkney trolls live in holes in the ground and have to be treated with respect and well spoken of, for to cross them would be most unwise.

Some human beings had powers or gifts of an uncanny nature. Possessors of the evil eye were said to be able to destroy people or cattle at will. Their victims had to go to great lengths to break the spells. The second sight was a faculty many dreaded having, for it almost invariably meant that premonitions of death, in the form of funeral processions or grey, misty shrouds, would pass in visions before their eyes.

The idea of death was never far from the minds of people living hard lives in a harsh environment. When it came it was treated with respect and accorded ceremonial. The dead person would be watched over for days by close friends and neighbours, while people from a wide area came to see and touch the corpse as a mark of respect. Sometimes a plate of salt was laid on the dead person's chest. The men would carry the coffin on their shoulders, often for miles, to its resting place in the family burial ground. Great importance was attached to returning the dead to lie beside their forebears. This may have sprung from a racial memory going back to the time of the great chambered cairns. In many places one can still trace the old funeral roads, with the small cairns marking the spots where the bearers stopped for rest and refreshment. In the Hebrides every township had a mourning-woman—*bean-tiurim*—who would walk behind the coffin intoning a lament. Mostly the women stayed to comfort the bereaved and to prepare food for the men on their return from the burial ground.

If death received its due of ceremony, so did other events in human life. News of a birth, the great sign of survival, was greeted everywhere with eager delight. A silver coin would be pressed into the small hand by every visitor. If the infant gripped it he would prosper, it was said. There were sometimes fears of a changeling being substituted for the real child by the fairy folk. People still living can remember the time when women of a certain Highland community would put a drop of water from a 'font' hidden deep in a wood into the baptismal bowl, to ensure protection against such a misfortune. This particular fear may have derived from prehistoric times when members of the tribe would try to steal healthy infants born to an enemy tribe, substituting their own weakly offspring, thus boosting the vitality of their own people.

The fostering of a chief's son by another member of the clan was common practice in older times. This was just another aspect of the oneness of the clan which gave the Highlanders a deep sense of security. In the Northern Isles, after the introduction of the feudal system in the sixteenth century under the Stewart earls, the people held land from immigrant Scottish tacksmen, but their allegiance was still to Norse ways. This gave them a certain solidarity though, without the close ties of the clan, they lived basically to a more independent pattern.

Customs and beliefs, however, were very similar over the whole crofting area. An early crofter from Harris would no doubt have settled quite easily into the life of one on Fetlar, though there might have been certain language problems. A celebration in which they would all have joined with enthusiasm was the wedding feast. This was an occasion for which all families with daughters had to be well prepared. The period of courtship would end with the asking, when the suitor, armed with a bottle of whisky, would call one evening at the house of his intended. After the usual exchange of remarks about the weather, the state of the crops or the fishing and so on, he would bring the conversation round to the important matter of seeking the parents' consent to the marriage. Then, with the wedding fixed, for a lucky day such as a Tuesday or Thursday, in a time of waxing moon, preparations started in earnest. The whole community took part, contributing eggs, cheese, poultry, perhaps a slaughtered sheep, huge bakings of bannocks and gallons of whisky. On the wedding morning a white flag was flown from the roof of the bride's house and she set off in procession with her party to meet the groom's party at the church or manse. After the ceremony and breaking of the wedding bannock over the bride's head, there was feasting and dancing in the decorated barn to the music of fiddle and box. The celebrations went on for several days and nights till the food and drink ran out and exhaustion overtook the guests.

These times of revelry were without doubt therapeutic. It was impossible to keep Celt or Norseman from indulging his capacity for enjoyment from time to time. He had to outshout the wind and outdance the wildest wave to prove his fitness for survival!

In many parts of the Highlands there was another way of marrying — at the handfasting stone. This was a holed stone, often situated in a remote place, at which a couple would meet and, after clasping hands through the hole, in the presence of witnesses, would declare themselves married, or betrothed, which was the equivalent — for a year and a day. If at the end of that time they found they were unsuited, or no child had been born, they were free to break the contract. This custom anticipated current lifestyles!

Indeed, as one looks as closely as is possible through records and documents at the lives of early crofters, one is struck not by the quaintness of their ways but by the clear-sighted inventiveness and adaptability to environment which are surely the marks of the modern outlook. I have heard of a man living in a high strath near Glen Urquhart, a hundred years ago, who put underfloor heating into his kitchen by means of hot-air ducts leading from his peat fire.

Through sons serving as soldiers in America or India and others sailing the seven seas, the people had contacts with many parts of the world and were always anxious for news. When they were given the chance of adequate schooling they were able to develop their mental capacities to the full. It is said that the greatest export from the Orkney islands has been university professors.

Towards the end of the eighteenth century the Scottish Society for the Propagation of Christian Knowledge had begun to establish schools in the Highlands as part of the movement to 'civilise' the people and ensure the end of rebellion. Some of the early teachers had a difficult task persuading parents to accept what looked like patronage, but, as time went on and it became clear that benefits were accruing, most people were glad enough to have their children taught, with the proviso that they might stay at home to help with seasonal work such as sowing, peat-cutting and harvesting. The schoolmaster often doubled as catechist and preacher and came to be a respected member of the community. The people would undertake to renew his roof thatch each year, he had the keep of a cow and the pupils each brought a peat every day for the schoolroom fire.

After the Education Act of 1872, which made schooling compulsory, Gaelic was strongly discouraged in the schools. Parents themselves wished children to abandon it as English was considered the passport to prosperity in the shape of work and wages in other parts. Only today is it being realised that the loss of this marvellously expressive language is a tragedy and efforts are being made to reinstate it by teaching at all levels.

The more highly educated the sons and daughters of crofting communities became the more they felt it essential to keep in touch with their forebears. Today it is the Canadian professors, the doctors from Peru, the business-men from Hong Kong and the Cambridge undergraduates who come to look at the scattered stones beside the shiny bungalow in a field in Skye and to finger the flowered porridge bowl on the shelf by the electric fire. There is soundness still in the inherited outlook. Many of those who have tasted success in various fields in many parts of the world would give anything for a return to the uncomplicated life of those still engaged in crofting. But return is not easy.

Crofting Today—and Tomorrow

It is now nearly 200 years since the first crofts were established. Today they number about 15,000, varying in size from one to a hundred acres. There have been great changes, brought about by mechanisation, the opening of communications by new roads and bridges, the growth of welfare and education services, the coming of radio and television. All the developments of the modern world have impinged upon the crofting communities, yet the remarkable thing is that in many places the way of life has changed so little. It is still possible, even on the mainland, to go into a small house, corrugated iron covering the thatch, to be welcomed with a kindly Gaelic greeting and led to a seat by a peat fire. A *strupach* will be offered, or a dram should occasion demand it, and the man and woman of the house, however busy they may be, will always find time for a 'news'. The conversation will range from the state of the weather and the crops and livestock to affairs in the country as a whole and the latest turn of events on the world scene.

In the northern part of the Applecross Peninsula it is only within the last few years that there has been more than a footpath linking croft to croft. In the Uists, in the month of May, one can find a whole family, clad in jeans and tee-shirts, engaged in planting potatoes in the age-old way. The making of the lazy-bed, the only appropriate form of cultivation in the tiny patches of earth between the rocks, is now done with a sharp, steel-bladed spade, instead of the *cas chrom*. Seaweed is barrowed in, as it always was—why pay the high cost of imported chemicals when wrack is on the doorstep? The wooden rake breaks the clods on the strips of earth that will not take the harrow.

The croft will not be the whole means of subsistence for the family. As in former times, it will not be much more than a base, but a supply of potatoes and other vegetables (I have eaten carrots and cauliflower grown on the machair in Harris which would have graced the pages of a seed catalogue!), eggs and milk, butter and cheese goes at least halfway towards keeping the household fed.

The man of the house may be a full-time fisherman or he may have one of the service jobs that are now available as the crofting communities emerge into the modern world—as postman, bus-driver or pier-master. His sons may find work in a seaweed-processing plant or a newly developed industry such as fish-farming, or in construction. For his daughters there are now jobs near home, as shop assistants or in the offices and canteens at Service bases, construction yards and so on. In the areas of oil exploration and of platform building there is obviously work of many different kinds, skilled and unskilled. With piped water and electricity in most of the

houses now, men and women are relieved of the time-consuming drudgery of many daily chores and free to give their energy to gainful employment. In most places there are openings in various kinds of forestry work and in the construction of roads, bridges, houses and other buildings.

It is not always realised that half the land area of Scotland, or one-sixth of Great Britain, lies in the crofting counties. Since the Act of 1886 there have been fears that with these large tracts subdivided into uneconomically small units and in the hands of protected tenants, many of whom were averse to change, there would be stagnation in the land. The crofter's aversion to change is understandable when one remembers what change meant to his forefathers prior to the Act. In fact, there had been a growing tendency for ambitious crofters to purchase their holdings when this was possible, perhaps at the break-up of an estate, when as sitting tenants they bought them at a reasonable price. As small landowners they could then dictate the pace and the kind of change that suited them. Still most of the crofting lands remained in the hands of tenants whose average age tended to grow steadily greater as the young men moved away to find paid work. Now, however, this hanging on by the old men may prove a blessing. As the possibility of finding good jobs near at hand becomes gradually more real, the young can claim their rightful inheritance without the fear of the insecurity which haunted their fathers.

That there is a demand by the young for a return to the independence and fulfilment of making a life on one's own terms is a fact today. If enough young people are able to make this return to an area then real revitalisation will take place. As things are there is a lot of social life even in what seem remote places. The old spirit of interdependence and togetherness is by no means dead. With modern transport the inhabitant of the last house in the strath can reach meetings of the 'Rural' or a gathering in the church hall. An influx of young families would mean the reopening of the local school, perhaps the appointment of a district nurse, the establishment of a community centre, a shop and so on.

The setting up of the Highlands and Islands Development Board in 1965 was, it was hoped, going to be a step in the right direction. The Crofters' Commission had done much to improve crofting conditions by making grants for reclamation, loans and advisory services available. But the Board, as it came to be known, had as its main aim the provision of jobs in industry. In its first report, in 1967, it said: 'Crofting ... if one had to look now for a way of life which would keep that number of people in relatively intractable territory, it would be difficult to contrive a better system. But its future depends on other employment support. This the Board accepts as a clear challenge and duty.'

In the last twelve years it has helped to finance schemes for food-processing, building contracting, motor repairs and so on. It has also encouraged a wide range of craft projects such as pottery and weaving. What is considered perhaps its most important contribution to development has been assistance to fishery, by way of loans and grants for the purchase of boats, training of young entrants to the industry and setting up boatyards, fish farms, marine-engineering shops and so on.

The Board itself appears to attach a good deal of importance to tourism as an adjunct to crofting. It is the only industry which can be developed right on the doorsteps of the remoter communities. Grants and loans are available for provision of additional accommodation, catering and other facilities for holiday visitors in the croft houses or in chalets and on camp sites.

The crofting community has always been in the habit of welcoming the stranger and there is no pleasanter place on earth for the weary traveller than a seat at a peat fire or at a table laden with fresh produce. But the crofter, as an agriculturalist, even a part-time one, does not relish the prospect of a constant stream of people of all kinds tramping about his place, poking into byre and barn, climbing fences, strewing plastic rubbish for calves to choke on, leaving gates open, disturbing stock. When autumn comes and he can put his feet up at his own fireside he gives a certain sigh of relief.

So how is the problem, which is really the Highland problem, to be solved? More and more people, scientists, sociologists and industrialists among them, are coming to the conclusion that the answer has been there all along. The thing to do is what has always been done—to make use of the resources which lie to hand in the way appropriate to those resources, that is to say, not to try to attract industry or large numbers of visitors to areas where these things and people cannot be accommodated, but to develop the natural assets of the various localities in natural ways. In former times resources were not exploited, but husbanded with care. Frank Fraser Darling, in his chapter on the ecology of land use in *The Future of the Highlands*, says: 'While the Hebrideans were dependent on the environment for their whole subsistence a very beautiful ecological adaptation to circumstances took place. . . . When a culture is beginning to break down, its disciplines of existence also begin to fail and the empirical conservation of habitat at which the people had arrived breaks down to exploitative attrition of natural resources.'

Exploitative attrition can be avoided before it is too late. On the west mainland there are places, such as Inverewe, where the Gulf Stream brings climatic conditions suitable for growing plants even of tender habit. Market-gardening could be an appropriate activity here. In Shetland, fishing was in an excellent state before the discovery of oil and is likely to be so, given a fair chance, after the wells have run dry. In Orkney, beef production and dairying can be as important as fishing. In the Western Isles fishing, also, is developing and much land reclamation can and is being undertaken. The machair lands, on the Atlantic coasts, consist of wind-blown shell sand. One has only to see the incredible profusion of wild flowers covering them in spring to judge of their fertility. What is needed for all these island communities, and for the more remote mainland ones, is sufficient subsidising of communications, provision of adequate boat and ferry services and a reduction in freight charges. Unless these things are done the cost of living and trying to make a living in the far-off places will be prohibitive.

In this connection it is interesting to see what is being done in northern Norway. Roads and bridges and adequate ferry services are being provided for the remoter islands, with the result that the young people are flocking back, small towns are growing up and education, even to university level, is being provided. Would the idea of universities, or at least colleges of advanced learning in Lerwick, Kirkwall, Stornoway and Inverness be an impossible dream?

The people of the Highlands and the Islands are making their voices heard today. This is part of the wide movement of self-determination of minorities. They know themselves —who better?—what is needed to make their lives productive and secure. Shetland deals very adequately with its own affairs. The Western Isles have their own Islands Council. There are real signs of the times in the setting up of community co-operatives, sponsored by the Highland Board, such as those on Vatersay (an island coming into its own at last), Eriskay, Harris, Papa Westray in Orkney, Park and Ness in Lewis. This last was registered in June 1978 and has issued its first annual report. Its activities include opening an office and a shop, acquisition of building land, bulk purchase of feeding stuffs and fertilisers, market gardening, provision of a mobile snack bar, council house construction and hiring out of heavy agricultural equipment. Both the Crofters' Commission and the Highland Board are anxious to encourage suitable enterprises and have issued a leaflet outlining the opportunities for development and mentioning other agencies which can provide financial assistance, such as the Highland Fund, the Shetland Trust and the Lewis Development Fund.

The current mood of discontent with urban living has brought a demand for crofts, in many cases from people who have no experience and very little idea of what a croft is. The word is often thought to mean the house, instead of the land. The Crofters' Commission has published a pamphlet explaining briefly the definition of a croft, how to acquire one and so on, for the benefit of such applicants. The present high rate of house prices, especially in the south, has generated such sizeable offers for croft properties as to create an almost irresistible temptation to sell for some people who see themselves, for the first time in their lives, with a desirable asset on their hands. It should be noted, however, that there has not been a rush by tenant crofters to buy their homes, many of them preferring to remain under the protection of the existing regulations.

If the houses which are sold become holiday homes then this is a short cut to depopulation. Townships become ghost settlements for the greater part of the year. In winter, when neighbours are most needed, there is hardly one in sight. No children means no school, the shop-cum-post office closes

for lack of trade, the bus ceases to run, a standstill is imposed. If the new owners are permanent residents who intend to take employment in the area or to set up small enterprises in crafts such as weaving or woodwork, then their coming can be beneficial. But too often such people do not consider carefully the implications of their venture and are not prepared for all that is involved in taking up a life of comparative isolation, so that their enterprises do not always succeed.

What is really needed is for the descendants of the original crofting stock to find their way back to the croft lands, not as retired pensioners but as people at the start of life. There are signs that this is happening. To be one's own master, making one's own decisions, to live in the freedom of hill and sea must always be attractive to the young. Now more than ever, the value of such living is being realised.

The European Economic Commission lately proposed a development for the Western Isles which would provide £20 million, half to come from the British Government and half from the Common Market. But a report from the Economic and Social Committee of the European Communities points out that, in order to qualify for such aid, there would have to be large-scale amalgamations of holdings and such amalgamations would disrupt the existing socio-economic systems. The Committee do not believe the Islanders should be forced to change their way of life which has been determined by history, culture and economic realities. The report states that 'These activities are essential to the economy and social stability of the area'.

In this connection the Crofters' Commission has pointed out that the present system holds the population and involves a fairly intensive use of relatively poor land. The emergence of community co-operatives shows that the crofters are capable of initiative and enterprise. Larger holdings might be more vulnerable economically. The Commission believes that 'the crofting system has considerable social, cultural, linguistic and economic importance at the national and indeed European level. It would be a very great loss—and would have almost unthinkable consequences—if the system were to be threatened seriously by artificial inducements to amalgamation in the pursuance of structural improvement.'

It is good to hear the people on the ground stating thus clearly a case for the retention of something so intangible yet of such incalculable value as a way of life. One hopes that will be the last word on the subject, the enduring verdict.